You Can Do It!

Prompt Like a Pro

101 High Impact Prompts *for Fiction and Nonfiction Authors*

A COMPANION BOOK
For *AI for Authors*

Karen Hodges Miller

Open Door Publications

Prompt Like a Pro
101 High Impact Prompts
for Fiction and Nonfiction Authors

ISBN: 979-8-9871697-9-7

Printed in the United States of America

Published by
Open Door Publications
Willow Spring, NC
www.OpenDoorPublications.com

For Kaylee, Jack, and Madison, who will grow up using software and computers in ways we haven't even thought of yet.

Contents

A Note About AI Use in This Book

This is a book about Artificial Intelligence (AI). I used several AI apps in working on it because how else should one check if details about AI are correct but with an AI chatbot?

I also used Claude Sonnet for research, I often consult Grammarly, I've been experimenting with Sudowrite, and my little AI robot was created with ChatGPT.

Part 1

Why
Prompting Matters

Chapter 1

Garbage In, Gold Out

Artificial intelligence is not magic.

I should know. In another writing life, I write paranormal romance. I spend a great deal of time inventing witches, elves, werewolves, curses, magical artifacts, and the occasional supernatural disaster. In my latest book I even added computers in a new magical combination called "technomancy," and instead of a screen they use something called the "Aether Array." AI is nothing like that, though I often wish it was.

Unfortunately, we still have to work in the real world, and while AI sometimes feels as if you are talking with a rather magical friend who is available at any time day or night, and can actually read your mind, AI isn't magic.

It isn't a crystal ball. It isn't prophecy. It isn't some enchanted library hidden beneath a mountain where wise spirits wait to answer your questions. And it certainly can't read your mind.

AI is a tool.

And like every other tool that writers use, from spellcheck to story structure software, it works best in skilled hands. That thought may intimidate you. You may have automatically thought, "Well I'm not skilled at this fancy computer stuff; I can barely use Google Docs," the good news is that learning to use an AI tool to help you with your writing is easy. Trust me, if I can learn this, so can you.

The most surprising thing I learned while researching my first book on Artificial Intelligence, *AI for Authors,* was not which chatbot performed best or which editing software had the most features. It was that the most disappointing AI results are not caused by weak software, they are caused by weak prompts. That simple realization changed how I use AI.

Like many writers, my early experiments were a mix of excitement and frustration. Sometimes the software produced something useful. Other times it gave me generic advice, research I couldn't trust, or out and out "hallucinations." (That's a special term in the AI world meaning your AI software has gone awry and made something up from whole cloth.)

My first instinct was to blame the software. It would have been easier.

Writers have a long tradition of blaming tools. We blame pens that skip, printers that jam, computers that crash, and editors who tell us our favorite chapter has to go. AI forced me to admit something uncomfortable: sometimes the problem was me.

I asked vague questions. I gave incomplete instructions. I expected the software to read my mind.

It couldn't. It's not magic.

You're Probably Already Using AI

If you are a working author in the twenty-first century, there is a good chance you are already using artificial intelligence whether you realize it or not.

Maybe you run your manuscript through Grammarly. Maybe you use software that analyzes pacing or sentence variety. Maybe you ask a chatbot for title ideas. Maybe you use AI to brainstorm newsletter topics, summarize research, design graphics, or help write marketing copy.

If you use Google, you've probably noticed in the last year or so, the first answer you often get is in "AI Mode."

It's all AI, whether you know it or not.

I am not suggesting you replace your editor, your proofreader, your cover artist, your beta readers, and your own judgment with a chatbot.

Please do not do that, but AI can help you:

- Brainstorm faster.
- Organize ideas.
- Analyze structure.
- Catch obvious mistakes.
- Explore alternatives.
- Handle repetitive tasks.

Think of it this way. Imagine being a modern-day mechanic who refuses to use a diagnostic scanner. Could you still repair cars? Of course. Mechanics did it for decades. But modern vehicles contain computers, sensors, and systems that benefit from modern tools.

Writing is changing in the same way. You do not need every tool. You do not need to love every tool. However, you do need to understand what is available.

And most importantly, you need to know how to talk to it.

Garbage In, Garbage Out

There is an old saying in technology, "Garbage in, garbage out." In other words, bad information produces bad results. AI is especially vulnerable to this.

Look at these prompts:

Weak Prompt: *Make this better.*

You may think that you have asked the right question, but

once again, no matter which AI software you use, it can't read your mind. What, exactly, did you mean by "better?"

Do you need to improve your grammar? Are you worried your pacing is too slow? Are you afraid your "romantic" scene is falling flat or the frightening scene in your new horror novel just isn't scary enough?

Sometimes we need to make something shorter, sometimes it needs to be longer. A blurb for your Amazon listing might be longer than one designed for a Facebook page.

The software has no idea exactly what you mean by "better."

Now compare the first prompt with this:

Stronger Prompt: *Act as a developmental editor. Review this chapter for pacing issues. Identify three slow sections without changing plot events.*

Suddenly the request has direction.

Here is another example:

Weak Prompt: *Help me market my book.*

Stronger Prompt: *Suggest three newsletter ideas for readers of a cozy mystery featuring a history professor, his librarian girlfriend, and her dog. Limit suggestions to ideas that can be created in under two hours.*

See the difference? The first prompt asks for everything. The second asks for something specific. Specificity creates clarity. And clarity improves results.

The First Answer Is Rarely the Best

One of the biggest mistakes new AI users make is accepting the first response. New users often treat AI as an authority. Experienced users treat it as a collaborator. The difference is simple: beginners accept answers, experienced writers question them.

Think about working on the first draft of a book. You would not write Chapter One and immediately upload it to Amazon.

At least, I hope you wouldn't. Instead, you revise, edit, cut and paste, rewrite. You complain. You eat chocolate. Then you revise again.

AI should work the same way. Treat the first answer as a draft, not a destination.

Apply simple refinement methods whenever results feel weak.

Step One: Assign a Role. Tell AI who it should be. For example:

- Act as a developmental editor.
- Respond as a copy editor.
- Act as a romance writing coach.
- Review this as a marketing consultant.

Changing the role changes the feedback.

Step Two: Add Constraints. Good prompts narrow focus. For example:

- Limit suggestions to three. (This is a favorite constraint of mine; AI can often flood you with too much information.)
- Do not alter plot events.
- Keep the heroine's personality intact.
- Focus only on pacing.

Constraints reduce confusion.

Step Three: Ask for Critique: Do not be afraid to challenge the response. Try:

- Identify weaknesses in your previous answer.

- Where was this too general?
- What assumptions did you make?

Remember, you can critique AI. I'm often amused by the AI software's response when I do question it. For example, I told AI I was using that as an editor, I felt it used the word "particular" too much in its answers. It responded it was aware it used the word as an "easy go-to phrase." It did not, however, stop its overuse of that "particular" word. So much for training my AI. Sometimes, it is rather like training my cats!

Step Four: Request Alternatives. Sometimes the first answer is not wrong, it is merely average, or simply not right for you. Try one of these:

- Provide two stronger versions.
- Offer a more emotional rewrite.
- Give a concise alternative.
- Increase tension without changing events.

AI improves when you guide it. Serious authors do not settle for first drafts. Not from themselves. And not from machines.

Your AI Is Not the Author

This may be the most important thing you take away from this book. AI is your assistant. You are the author. AI can:

- Organize information.
- Suggest alternatives.
- Help brainstorm ideas.
- Analyze structure.
- Help identify problems.

AI cannot:

- Live your experiences.
- Understand your readers.
- Replace intuition.
- Make artistic decisions.
- Create your voice.

This last one is the most important. Your voice is your fingerprint. It is the reason readers choose your books instead of someone else's. Protect it.

Use AI to strengthen your writing. Do not let it flatten it.

Anatomy of a Strong Prompt

The most effective prompts contain five pieces.

- Goal
- Context
- Role
- Constraints
- Output

Let's break that down. A weak version of your prompt would be: *fix this chapter.* A stronger version includes the five parts listed above: *Act as a developmental editor to help me improve the pacing in my suspense novel. Do not change the plot events. Identify three slow sections and suggest improvements.*

Here is the prompt broken down:

- **Goal:** Improve the pacing.
- **Context:** suspense novel.
- **Role:** Developmental editor.
- **Constraints:** Do not change the plot events.
- **Output:** Identify three slow sections and suggest

improvements.

You made the same request and received a better result. This structure works both for fiction and for nonfiction. It also works for editing, marketing, outlining, and research.

We will use this structure repeatedly throughout this book.

Common Prompt Mistakes

If your results disappoint you, ***check the prompt first.***

Common problems include:

- Being too vague.
- Forgetting role assignment.
- Giving no constraints.
- Accepting the first answer.
- Asking for too much at once.
- Failing to ask follow-up questions.

The prompt, "*Help me write my book,*" is almost impossible to answer well. By changing it just a little bit, "*Act as a developmental editor. Help me identify three emotional weaknesses in my protagonist's arc for a paranormal romance involving witches and vampires.*"

Now you have something useful!

Clear prompts create clear results. Vague prompts create vague answers. Great prompts create better books.

Exercise

Take this prompt: ***Help me write my book.***

Rewrite it using:

- Goal
- Context
- Role
- Constraints
- Desired Output

Save your prompt. You will use it again in later exercises in this book. Before we talk about to whom to write advanced prompts, marketing prompts, editing prompts, or research prompts, you must first need to learn *how* to ask better questions.

Chapter 2
The Skeleton of a Great Prompt

Chapter One showed better prompts create better results. In Chapter Two we roll up our sleeves and learn how to build them. Think of a prompt like building a house. You can decorate the house. You can paint it, add fancy trim, install fancy countertops, and put flowers in its window boxes, but if the frame underneath is weak, the whole thing leans sideways.

Prompts work exactly the same way.

Many new AI users believe good prompting is some sort of mysterious talent possessed by "tech people." They imagine expert users typing strange commands like the "technomancers" in my fantasy novel. Luckily, it's much easier than that.

Most strong prompts are surprisingly ordinary. They simply contain enough information for AI to understand:

- What you want.
- Why you want it.
- How you want it done.
- What limits exist.
- What form the answer should take.

That's it. Five pieces. You already saw them briefly in Chapter One. Now we are turning them into a working system.

Goal: Tell AI What You Want

This sounds obvious. It isn't. Somehow, that's often not what we do when we begin a "conversation" with AI. Too often we begin by expecting the AI chatbot to know exactly what we are thinking. Don't forget; it's a chatbot, not a mind reader.

Here's an example of a weak prompt. *Hi Chatbot (many people I know name their AI) I need help with my novel.*

And yes, I can understand beginning your conversation in the same way you would begin speaking with a human friend. It's the way we have been taught to communicate, and it helps us feel more comfortable. But it doesn't help the AI.

In fact, AI will probably answer in the same way your human friend would—*So, exactly what do you need?*

Help with my novel is very, very broad. Help how? With plot? With dialogue? How about marketing and reader engagement? Or do you need to work on the basics, such as cleaning up grammar?

Here's a much stronger way to ask that prompt: *Help me improve the tension between two rivals in my young adult sports book.*

Now the software knows what success looks like. Stating your goal is like giving AI a destination on a GPS. Instead of driving in circles, AI now has a purpose.

Before asking AI for help, first define your goal by asking yourself: *What problem am I trying to solve?* You might want to improve your pacing, brainstorm titles, strengthen emotional conflict, analyze character motivation, or a host of other items every author needs to think about.

The clearer the goal, the better the response.

Context: Tell AI What It is Looking at

Context answers the question *What exactly are we working on?* Suppose you type: *Fix this scene.* That opens an entire world of possibilities for AI. Instead, try something like this: *Fix this scene from my urban fantasy romance involving witches and werewolves in a small Kentucky town. Preserve romantic tension and supernatural elements.*

That prompt changes everything. Context gives AI a map. Without it, the software just guesses what you mean. With context, it can collaborate with you.

Context may include:

- Genre
- Audience
- Character type
- Tone
- Series information
- Reader expectations
- Book purpose

For example, in fiction try something like: *This is a cozy mystery set in a small town in the Midwest in present day.*

If you are writing nonfiction, the context might be: *I'm working on a book that teaches self-publishing strategies for indie authors.*

If your question is about marketing, explaining the context is obviously important. Tell your AI to give you information about readers who are looking for books like yours. *Who are the target readers for a nonfiction self-help book for survivors of cancer?*

Context reduces randomness, and randomness is rarely your friend.

Role: Tell AI Who It Should Be

This one is fun; it's like asking AI to play dress-up with you. Instead of saying: *Review this chapter,* try this: *Act as a developmental editor and review this chapter for pacing problems.* Or, *Act as a marketing consultant and suggest three ways for me to increase my email newsletter mailing list.*

Changing the role of AI changes perspective. Think of it this way: you would not ask your dentist to repair your car. You would not ask your mechanic to perform surgery.

Different jobs. Different points of view. And the great thing is, with AI, one piece of software can help with multiple tasks.

Some common roles authors use are:

- Developmental editor
- Copy editor
- Line editor
- Beta reader
- Story coach
- Character analyst
- Worldbuilding consultant

Authors also need other types of assistance. Try asking AI to answer in a variety of other roles including:

- Marketing advisor
- Newsletter strategist
- Amazon listing consultant
- Research assistant

Constraints: Telling AI What NOT to Do

Writers often tell AI what they want, but they forget to explain the boundaries. Telling AI what information you don't want is just as important as telling it what you do want.

Very broad questions give AI too little information. For example, if you say: *Improve this chapter,* AI might rewrite your Point of View, change your character's motivation, rearrange events, or remove a favorite scene. None of which you wanted.

That's why you need to be more specific, or in "AI speak," add constraints. Instead of: *Improve this chapter,* ask, *Improve pacing without changing plot events or character personalities.* Limit suggestions to three areas.

Useful constraints include:

- Do not change plot events.
- Preserve my voice.
- Limit suggestions to three.
- Keep under 300 words.
- Focus only on dialogue.
- Avoid spoilers.
- Maintain historical accuracy.

Constraints reduce chaos. And yes, I love the "limit it to three" rule. AI can become extremely enthusiastic. Sometimes *too* enthusiastic. Ask it for ideas, and suddenly you have forty-seven suggestions, three subcategories, a bonus section, and an existential crisis.

I've even explained to my AI that I become anxious and nervous when given too many items to focus on. Now, it remembers that and refers to it in our chats on marketing. It will say something like: *To help keep your anxiety under control, we will only focus on one month at a time.*

I love a thoughtful AI.

Output: Tell AI What the Answer Should Look Like

Imagine asking a contractor to build you a kitchen. You never mention size. Or style. Or color. Or budget. You simply say, "Build something nice." You would be terrified of the results. Working with AI can feel the same way.

For example: *Help me edit this* is much too broad. Instead, a better prompt would be: *Identify three pacing problems and explain why they slow the chapter.*

Or: *Help market my book*, versus *Provide five newsletter ideas in bullet format suitable for a young-adult romance audience.*

You may prefer bullet lists to paragraphs, tables to summaries, or rewrites to critiques. Output determines shape. Goal determines destination. Together they create useful prompts.

Putting It Together

Here's the first draft of your prompt: *Help me with my story.* Now we add the pieces.

- **Goal:** Strengthen tension
- **Context:** Paranormal romance
- **Role:** Developmental editor
- **Constraints:** Do not change plot events
- **Output:** Identify three weak scenes

Your final prompt looks like this:

Act as a developmental editor. Review this paranormal romance chapter for emotional tension problems. Do not alter plot events. Identify three scenes that feel emotionally weak and suggest improvements.

Use this formula repeatedly:

Goal + Context + Role + Constraints + Output

Write it somewhere. A sticky note. Your notebook. On your computer screen. A tattoo is unnecessary.

Probably.

Exercise

Take one real writing problem from your current project. Fill in:

- Goal:
- Context:
- Role:
- Constraints:
- Output:

Now build the full prompt. Save it. You will use it again. Because next we move beyond structure and begin learning something even more powerful:

How wording changes results.

Chapter 3
Words Matter

By now you know prompts have structure. You know they need goals, context, roles, constraints, and output. You've built a prompt skeleton. However, the skeleton can't go very far without some muscle.

Something that surprises many new AI users is how small wording changes can produce dramatically different results. When I first started working with AI, I noticed I got different types of answers when I thought I was asking the same question.

Humans say the same thing in many different ways. "Let's get something to eat," can mean something very broad. "Let's go out to dinner," is slightly more precise. But "Let's go to the mall and get a pizza at that new restaurant," is much more detailed.

AI often responds more literally and directly than humans do. Think of the difference in the phrase, "What do you think about this sentence?" versus "Please check that the grammar in this sentence is correct."

Now think about the jargon, colloquialisms, and slang you use, and you can start to see why your AI prompts need to be precise.

One extra sentence, or one changed or removed instruction, can shift an answer you receive.

Different wording can yield different results.

When using prompts with AI, the words you choose

influence what the software notices, what it prioritizes, and how it responds.

Prompting is not merely asking questions; it is directing AI's attention.

Broad Questions Produce Broad Answers

Let's start with a simple example. Here's a weak prompt: *Tell me about book marketing.*

That question is enormous. Marketing where? For what type of book? For fiction? Nonfiction? Traditional publishing? Self-publishing? Do you want to run Amazon ads? Use social media—and which type of social media are you interested in? Do you want to start an author website, add to your email newsletter list? AI has to guess. And when AI guesses, you often receive generic answers.

Now compare it to this stronger prompt: *Explain three marketing methods suitable for indie fantasy authors with small budgets. Limit suggestions to ideas that can be done in under five hours per week.*

Notice what changed. We added information about the audience, the budget, and time limits, as well as the number of suggestions.

Same topic. Better wording. Better outcome.

Verbs Matter

Compare these prompts: *Look at this chapter.*

- Versus: *Analyze this chapter.*
- Or: *Critique this chapter.*
- Or: *Rewrite this chapter.*
- Or: *Summarize this chapter.*

Those are not the same request. Many writers accidentally use vague verbs such as:

- Help.
- Fix.
- Improve.
- Make better.

Humans understand the slight differences between those words. AI needs clearer direction. Make sure you choose verbs with a clear purpose. Here are a few good verbs to use when asking your AI to edit your work:

- Analyze
- Critique
- Identify
- Compare
- Revise
- Expand

These verbs are good for discussing marketing:

- Suggest
- Generate
- Prioritize
- Evaluate
- Organize

Here are some "story verbs:"

- Strengthen
- Increase
- Deepen
- Heighten
- Foreshadow

The clearer the verb, the clearer the response.

Tone Changes Everything

Writers understand tone instinctively. AI can respond to tone, too. Suppose you ask, *Write a newsletter announcement for my new mystery novel.*

That's a perfectly acceptable prompt. Now change it. *Write a warm newsletter announcement that feels conversational and reader-focused.*

You've asked for a different tone; you'll get a different result.

Here's a different prompt for the same question. *Write a dramatic announcement emphasizing danger, romance, and mystery.*

Again, you've asked a different question, and you'll get a different answer.

You can guide tone by using words such as:

- Warm
- Professional
- Humorous
- Emotional
- Formal
- Friendly
- Suspenseful
- Playful
- Academic
- Encouraging

Voice matters. You don't want your newsletter to sound like corporate marketing copy. You want it to sound like *you.*

One Word Can Change the Entire Direction

Let me show you something interesting:

Prompt One: *Suggest character ideas for a witch protagonist.*

Prompt Two: *Suggest unusual character ideas for a witch protagonist.*

Prompt Three: *Suggest morally complicated character ideas for a witch protagonist.*

Prompt Four: *Suggest historically inspired character ideas for a witch protagonist.*

The topic never changed. The words did. Those words act like signposts telling AI where to travel.

Try adding words such as:

- Emotional
- Historical
- Cozy
- Dark
- Humorous
- Realistic
- Romantic
- High stakes

These modifiers help narrow your results. Think of them as lenses that change what AI notices.

Compare these prompt pairs:

Weak: *Help me with dialogue.*

Stronger: *Strengthen tension in dialogue between two rivals who secretly care about each other. Preserve subtext.*

Weak: *Give me marketing ideas.*

Stronger: *Suggest three email newsletter topics for readers of a crime novel involving a jewel heist.*

Weak: *Improve my blurb.*

Stronger: *Revise this Amazon blurb for stronger emotional hooks while preserving the original plot. Keep under 200 words.*

Weak: *Make this scene better.*

Stronger: *Increase romantic tension without changing events or point of view.*

Do you see the pattern? Good prompts reduce guessing.

Precision Beats Complexity

New AI users sometimes think advanced prompting means long or complex prompting. It doesn't. A shorter prompt with clear wording often beats a longer prompt filled with unnecessary instructions. Here is an example:

Long but weak: *Please help me with my story because I'm stuck and not sure what to do and maybe the pacing is wrong and perhaps the characters need work and I'm also wondering about the ending.*

Yes, that's probably how we feel, but it won't help your AI to help you. Here's a short but stronger prompt. *Review this fantasy chapter for pacing problems only. Identify two slow sections.*

This prompt is short, focused, and useful. Complexity is not the goal. Clarity is.

Ask for Priorities

I frequently suggest asking your AI to limit its answers to two or three points. ***Limiting the number is usually a strategy, not a statement that only that many problems exist.***

If you ask your AI to review something for pacing problems, as in the example above, and to identify two slow sections, you are not saying there are *only* two pacing problems. You are saying "Show me the two most important ones first." Asking the question in an open-ended way can confuse either the author, AI, or both.

If you leave the question open, "identify pacing problems," AI might return all major and minor issues, speculative issues or issues AI guesses might exist, or just give you twenty suggestions you don't need. You may end up buried in feedback.

Here's an example of a broad request: *Review this fantasy chapter for pacing problems.*

You can focus AI by using this prompt: *Review this fantasy chapter for pacing problems only. Identify the two most significant slow sections.*

Or try an expanded request: *Review this fantasy chapter for pacing problems. List all issues you find and rank them from major to minor.*

Quantity Changes Output, Too

- Identify **two** problems equals prioritization.
- Identify **five** problems gives you a broader review.
- Identify **all** problems give you a comprehensive scan.
- Identify the **most serious** problem brings more focus.
- Rank problems by **severity** organizes the issues.

You do not need to write the perfect prompt the first time, every time. Professional AI users rarely do. Instead, they refine their prompts.

Write a prompt. Review your answer. Adjust. Prompt again. You already do this as an author. It's like writing a first draft, revising, revising again, and again until you are satisfied you have your best work.

Prompting follows the same rhythm. Treat prompts as living documents. Change a word, add context, remove clutter, or try another version.

Small changes often create surprisingly big improvements.

Exercise

Take one prompt you wrote in Chapter Two.

Now improve it by changing:

1. The verb
2. The tone
3. One descriptive word
4. One constraint

Compare the results. Did the answer change? It probably did. Prompting is not only about structure. It is about language. As writers, we fortunately already work with language every day.

Next, we move into something even more practical: How to hold a conversation with AI instead of asking one question at a time.

Chapter 4

The Conversation Method

Many people imagine prompting as a single question followed by a single answer. Ask AI something. Receive the perfect information. Move on.

That certainly works sometimes, particularly if you are asking a simple question. Experienced AI users rarely work that way. They hold conversations.

Chapter Two gave you the parts of a prompt, and Chapter Three showed how wording changes results, this chapter explains what happens next. Real prompting is often a process of refinement. You ask. You review. You adjust. You ask again.

Writers already know this rhythm. You do not write one draft and publish it. You write. You revise. You edit. You polish.

Prompting works much the same way. Think of AI less as a search engine and more as a conversation partner. The first answer is often the beginning, not the end.

The Myth of the Perfect Prompt

New users often believe they must write the perfect prompt the first time, which stops many people from trying before they even begin. They spend ten minutes writing instructions when they could spend thirty seconds getting an answer and refining it.

Professional AI users rarely begin with perfection. Instead, they use what I call ***prompt layering.*** Here's how it works:

Prompt One: *Give me ideas for a historical novel about the Dust Bowl.*

Receive your response, look it over, and think about additional or different information you would like. Now, ask again.

Prompt Two: *Make the setting smaller and more isolated.*

Review and ask again.

Prompt Three: *Increase the tension between the protagonist who may lose his farm and the banker who is worried about the only town bank going under.*

Guess what—it's time to review and ask another question!

Prompt Four: *Add a mystery element involving missing stolen money.*

Nothing magical happened in this process. And here's where the human part—your part—of getting what you need from AI comes in. As you asked a question and reviewed the information you received, it triggered your brainstorming abilities. The first question gave you a simple setting. After thinking about it, you decided a small, isolated area could add more texture and layers to the story. As you narrowed your focus on your protagonist, a farmer, you began to think about his possible problems—Dust Bowl, dying crops, mortgage due. That's a pretty simple and obvious story line with the obvious antagonist being the evil banker who wants to foreclose. But let's make our antagonist more complex: he's trying to save the town.

You see where I'm going with this. Each question adds more layers to your thinking, leading to a new prompt, which adds a new layer.

Prompting is often a more efficient way of brainstorming. You build. You adjust. You continue.

Prompt Chains

A ***prompt chain*** is a sequence of prompts where each answer helps create the next step. Here is an example.

Prompt One: *Suggest five ideas for a contemporary romance set in a bakery in a small town.*

Prompt Two: *Take idea three and expand the heroine.*

Prompt Three: *Develop the love interest.*

Prompt Four: *Suggest three secrets that could create conflict.*

Prompt Five: *Outline the first three chapters.*

Notice what happened through the prompt chain. You did not ask for an entire novel. You built one piece at a time, stopped to review each answer, and added your own take on each of the ideas.

Prompt chains reduce overwhelm. They also improve quality because each step receives attention. Trying to do everything at once often creates shallow answers. Breaking work into stages usually creates stronger ones.

Narrow Before You Expand

Many authors, I admit I'm often one, expand before they narrow. Not just when using AI, but in thinking about their books.

They start here: *Help me plan my book.*

That prompt is enormous. Try moving through the story one piece at a time. Start with:

Prompt One: *Brainstorm the opening conflict.*

Then ask:

Prompt Two: *Identify the inciting incident that pushes the protagonist into action.*

Next:

Prompt Three: *Suggest three complications or obstacles.*

Then:

Prompt Four: *Identify a possible midpoint twist or revelation.*

Continue with:

Prompt Five: *Suggest two dark moments where the protagonist feels defeated.*

Then:

Prompt Six: *Suggest possible climaxes and resolutions.*

You can go even smaller.

Discuss:

- Character goal
- Character motivation
- Stakes
- Scene conflict
- Turning point
- Disaster or consequence
- Emotional arc
- Revelation
- Climax
- Resolution

Large projects become easier when divided into smaller tasks. AI works best when you give it manageable pieces. Writing often works the same way. Smaller prompts often produce bigger results. Think: Scene first. Then sequence. Then chapter. Then act. Then book.

Use Follow-Up Prompts

One of the biggest mistakes beginners make is accepting the first answer. Remember our discussion from the last chapter: wording changes output. Follow-up prompts change it even more.

Suppose AI gives you a scene outline.
Try asking:

- *Make this darker.*
- *Increase suspense.*
- *Reduce exposition.*
- *Preserve events but increase emotional tension.*
- *Add subtext.*
- *Keep the dialogue but raise conflict.*

Don't think of this as starting over. Think of it as brainstorming and editing. That is a very different mindset.

When AI Starts Asking Questions

Sometimes AI answers your prompt with another question. New users occasionally think something has gone wrong. It hasn't.

Often the AI is trying to gather missing information. Suppose you ask: *Help me market my memoir.*
AI might respond:

- *Who is the audience?*
- *What themes does the memoir cover?*
- *Is the tone inspirational, humorous, or reflective?*
- *Do you already have a newsletter?*

AI is not refusing to answer; it is gathering context. Remember back in Chapters 1 and 2 where we discussed:

- Goal
- Context
- Role
- Constraints
- Output

If those pieces are missing, AI may ask for them.

Writers can use this intentionally. Try prompts such as: *Before answering, ask me up to five questions that would improve your response.*

Or: *Interview me about this project before suggesting ideas.*

This works especially well for:

- Memoirs
- Nonfiction
- Worldbuilding
- Marketing plans
- Reader profiles
- Series development

While working on *The Elf Knight*, my latest book in my paranormal fantasy series, AI gave me a response related to the story canon. I pushed back. AI asked me why.

My answer was simple, *Because I didn't trust your response.*

That may sound strange in a book about prompting, but it is one of the most important lessons I can give you. Good AI users do not trust it automatically. They verify. They compare. They question.

In my situation, I knew the world. I knew the canon. I knew how my mysterious fog should behave, which characters held secrets, and which pieces of history mattered.

AI did not know those things unless I taught them. The problem was not that AI answered; the problem would have been accepting the answer without thinking.

Prompting is not obedience. It is collaboration. The best results often happen when you say:

- *That doesn't feel right.*
- *Why did you choose that?*
- *Show me another approach.*
- *This conflicts with earlier information.*

Professional users question the output because they are still the author, editor, researcher, and decision maker. AI is a tool. You are the expert.

You can even turn AI into an interviewer. Here's a prompt to try: *Act as a developmental editor. Ask questions one at a time to help me strengthen my protagonist.*

Or: *Interview me about my memoir before helping me organize chapters.*

Sometimes the best prompt is not an answer. It is a better question.

Ask for Priorities First

Earlier we discussed limiting answers. Consider these prompts.

Broad: *Review this chapter for pacing problems.*

Focused: *Review this chapter for pacing problems only. Identify the two most significant slow sections.*

Expanded: *Review this chapter for pacing problems. Rank issues from major to minor.*

Notice the difference. You are not saying only two problems exist. You are asking AI to prioritize. This keeps feedback manageable. It also prevents you from drowning in suggestions.

Writers receive enough opinions already. You do not need twenty more at once.

When AI Starts Guessing

Sometimes AI runs out of obvious problems. When that happens, it may begin offering possibilities instead of observations. You might see comments such as:

- *Readers may become confused.*
- *The romance might need strengthening.*
- *The ending could use more tension.*

Those suggestions are not necessarily wrong. But they are vague and they may not be supported by the text you wrote. Think of them as possibilities rather than facts. This is different than an AI "hallucination." This is your AI trying its best to give you the answer it thinks you asked for. We will talk more about AI "hallucinations" in Chapter Sixteen.

Experienced users learn to use more detail in their questions. *Show evidence from the chapter supporting this suggestion.* Or: *Identify only issues directly visible in the text.*

That simple instruction often improves accuracy.

The Revision Loop

Many professionals use some version of this process:

Step One: Create.

Step Two: Review.

Step Three: Refine.

Step Four: Repeat.

For example, Create a scene, review pacing, revise dialogue. Increase tension, check continuity, polish wording.

You already know this process. It is called writing. AI simply moves beside you.

Prompting is Conversation

Using prompts is simply having a conversation with your AI. You ask it a question. It responds. You think about its response and ask another question. Here's an example of a typical "prompt conversation:"

First prompt: *Suggest ideas for a cozy mystery involving a missing heirloom.*

Second prompt: *Take idea two and increase family conflict.*

Third prompt: *Add a historical connection.*

Fourth prompt: *Develop three suspects.*
Fifth prompt: *Create motives for each suspect.*
Sixth prompt: *Outline the opening chapters.*

AI doesn't require you to use words like "please" and "thank you," or to do anything more than ask a basic question. Most people are more comfortable with a conversational style that feels similar to speaking to another human. While I've kept my questions to the basics while writing this book, what I'd actually type would look more like this: *Good morning, I'm working on a new book idea today. Please suggest three ideas for a cozy mystery involving a missing family heirloom.*

Does this make your AI respond better? No. In fact, don't add too much "chat" when talking to your chatbot. It might only confuse it. A little more natural flow, however, can help you get into the conversational flow.

Exercise

Take one project you are currently working on.
Do **not** ask AI to solve the whole thing.
Instead break it into five smaller prompts.
Write them down and save them.

You have just created your first prompt chain.

Chapter 5
Prompt Recipes for Authors

We talked about how prompts work.
We've discussed structure. We've explored wording. We've learned how conversations improve results. Now it is time to do what writers always want to do: Use it.

Think of this chapter as your first prompt toolbox. These are not advanced prompts. They are not secret formulas known only to mysterious AI experts hidden in dark basements surrounded by blinking computer screens.

They are working prompts. Simple. Practical. Adaptable. You can change them, expand them, combine them, or use them exactly as written. Remember what we learned earlier: treat prompts as drafts. You do not need perfection, only a starting place.

Story and Brainstorming Prompts

Story ideas often begin as fragments. A phrase, a sentence, a character, a question. Maybe even a dream.

AI works well when you give it one piece and ask it to help you build the rest.

Try prompts such as:

- *Suggest three urban fantasy story ideas involving witches in a small Midwestern town. Include the central conflict and romantic tension.*

- *Act as a character coach. Help me deepen a paranormal heroine. Identify three strengths, two flaws, one fear, and one hidden motivation.*
- *Suggest three complications that could increase tension between a heroine and her rival without changing their personalities.*
- *Help me develop a magical community hidden inside a modern town. Include rules, dangers, and possible conflicts.*

Plot Development Prompts

Many writers freeze because they try to build an entire novel at once. Instead, work smaller. Ask about one piece at a time.

Try this opening prompt: *Suggest three possible opening conflicts for a cozy mystery involving a missing family heirloom.*

Or:

- *Identify an event that forces the protagonist into action.*
- *Suggest a midpoint revelation that changes the direction of the story.*
- *Create two moments where the protagonist feels defeated.*
- *Suggest possible climaxes while preserving the emotional arc.*

Editing Prompts

AI can help you review your writing. It should not replace your human editor. It can be used to identify possibilities.

Try prompts such as:

- *Act as a developmental editor. Review this chapter for pacing problems only. Identify the two most significant slow sections.*
- *Review dialogue for places where conflict could increase. Preserve character voice.*

- *Identify scenes where emotional stakes feel weak.*
- *Look for timeline or continuity issues visible in the chapter.*

Marketing Prompts

As authors we don't only write books, we market them, too. Often reluctantly. AI can help. Here are some marketing prompts:

- *Suggest three newsletter topics for readers of a historical mystery series.*
- *Review this Amazon description. Increase emotional hooks without changing plot details.*
- *Suggest reader magnet ideas for an urban fantasy romance series.*
- *Generate five short promotional posts suitable for Facebook.*

Research Prompts

Research is another area where AI can help. Carefully. Always verify the information you find. Check to make sure the links actually exist. Here are a few prompts to try:

- *List major social concerns in Virginia in the 1700s.*
- *Describe the daily work of a small-town librarian.*
- *Suggest details that would make a rural Southern town feel authentic.*
- *Help me build a chronology for this story.*

Productivity Prompts

Writers wear many hats. AI can help organize them. Try:

- *Create a revision checklist for a second draft.*
- *Build a launch task list for an indie author.*
- *Suggest a weekly writing schedule for someone with limited time.*

- *Help me divide this large project into smaller steps.*

Prompt Tip: Borrow First, Customize Later

New users sometimes worry they are "doing prompting wrong." You are not. Use examples. Steal structures. Change wording. Add context. Remove pieces.

The best prompt writers often begin with someone else's framework and make it their own. That is exactly what writers have always done.

Exercise

Choose one area:

- Brainstorming
- Plotting
- Editing
- Marketing
- Research
- Productivity

Write one prompt you could use today.
Save it.
You have just started building your personal prompt library.

In the next section we move from examples to complete prompt collections.

Part 2

Prompt Library

Using the Prompt Library

The first section of this book focused on *how* to work with AI. We explored why prompting is really a conversation, why the first response is rarely the final response, and how smaller, focused requests often produce better results than one enormous instruction.

Now we put these ideas into practice.

This section is your prompt library. Think of it as a toolbox rather than a script. You are not expected to use every prompt exactly as written. In fact, you probably should not. The prompts in these chapters are meant to be starting places, examples you can adjust, expand, shorten, combine, or rewrite to fit your own projects.

The library is organized by writing tasks and author needs. Fiction writers may use prompts for brainstorming ideas, developing characters, building worlds, increasing conflict, or strengthening scenes. Memoir writers may use prompts to uncover memories, identify themes, organize life events, and explore emotional threads. Nonfiction writers may focus on organization, research, explanations, audience needs, and reader takeaways.

In Part Three we move beyond drafting AI prompts for writing into the practical side of Authorpreneurship. You will find prompts for editing, revision, publishing tasks, marketing, and working with AI as an assistant rather than a replacement writer.

Not every prompt fits every author. A romance writer, memoirist, historian, business author, and fantasy novelist may all use AI differently. That is expected. The goal is not to force everyone into one process. The goal is to provide enough examples to help you begin building a prompt style that works for you.

Consider these prompts as ingredients. Mix them, modify them, break them apart, or combine them.

The best prompt you create in this book may end up being one you rewrite entirely. And that is exactly how it should work.

Chapter 6
Fiction Prompts

Fiction authors often worry AI will replace creativity.

It won't.

A prompt does not write imagination. It gives imagination somewhere to go. Used well, AI becomes a brainstorming partner, research assistant, developmental editor, and occasional sounding board. Used poorly, it becomes a random idea machine that throws twenty suggestions at you, none of which fit your book. The difference is usually the prompt. We will talk about this more in Chapter Nineteen.

This chapter contains prompts to help fiction writers develop stories without surrendering authorship. You remain the writer. AI becomes the assistant. Think of these prompts as starting places. Change genre. Change tone. Add your own world, characters, and themes. The more specific you become, the better the response usually becomes.

Story Idea and Concept Prompts

Prompt 1: The Story Spark

Prompt: *Suggest five story concepts for a [genre] novel featuring [character type]. Include the central conflict, emotional stakes, and possible setting.*

Add your own genre and character. This prompt asks for multiple ideas but limits the response to usable pieces such as character, conflict, stakes, and setting. Instead of *Give me story ideas*, you receive structured concepts.

Prompt 2: Opening Conflict Builder

Prompt: *Brainstorm three possible opening conflicts for a novel about [premise]. Include how each conflict could lead into a larger story problem.*

Let's say you are writing a historical romance set in 1944 in New York City; possible premises might be the Empire State Building, the New York Public Library. Possible outputs might include missing money, family scandal, wartime secrets. Small conflicts often become larger plots.

Prompt 3: Escalation Prompt

Prompt: *Given this premise, suggest three complications that increase tension without solving the story problem.*

This is excellent when writers become stuck in the middle of their plot.

Character Development Prompts

Prompt 4: Hidden Wound Prompt

Prompt: *Create a backstory "wound" for this character. Explain how it affects their goals, fears, and relationships.*

Characters become interesting when history collides with present action.

Prompt 5: Motivation Layers

Prompt: *List:*

- *External goal*
- *Internal goal*
- *Fear*

- *Misbelief*
- *Emotional need for this character.*

This mirrors many modern story methods and helps separate *want* from *need.*

Prompt 6: Opposing Character Prompt

Prompt: *Suggest an antagonist whose goals make sense from their point of view.*

Villains rarely wake up intending evil. Most believe they are right. In our minds, we are always the hero of our own story.

Plot and Structure Prompts

Brief note: Many plotting systems use slightly different language such as:

- Inciting Incident
- First Plot Point
- Midpoint Shift
- Dark Moment
- Climax
- Resolution

You do not need to know or use everything in a system, but knowing the vocabulary can help when prompting.

Prompt 7: Inciting Incident Generator

Prompt: *Suggest five inciting incidents for this story premise. Include how each changes the protagonist's ordinary world.*

Prompt 8: Midpoint Shift Prompt

Prompt: *Suggest a midpoint revelation that changes what* *the protagonist believes about the conflict.*

Prompt 9: Dark Moment Prompt

Prompt: *Brainstorm three "all is lost" moments for this novel.*

Worldbuilding Prompts

No matter what genre you are writing, your book has its own world. While we think of worldbuilding as something only used in fantasy or sci-fi, it is also an important part of any story, even memoir.

Prompt 10: Setting Expansion

Prompt: *Describe this setting using:*

- *sights*
- *sounds*
- *smells*
- *textures*
- *emotional atmosphere*

Prompt 11: Society Builder

Prompt: *Create customs, traditions, conflicts, and beliefs for this fictional community. Base it on (add a culture).*

This type of prompt is often the start of a discussion. AI suggests a tradition, you ask for more information. Or the suggestion sets off a train of other ideas. For example, when building the world for my book *The Elf Knight,* I wanted to explore both Nordic and Celtic elf myths. I asked for research on both groups.

Prompt 12: Hidden History Prompt

Prompt: *Suggest three historical events that shaped this* *world before the novel begins.*

Readers love the feeling that a world existed even before Chapter 1.

Scene Prompts

Prompt 13: Scene Expansion

Prompt: *Review this scene. Suggest places to increase conflict, emotion, tension, or sensory detail.*

Notice: We are asking for improvements and suggestions. Not for AI to rewrite the story.

Prompt 14: Dialogue Deepening

Prompt: *Review this dialogue scene and identify places where subtext could replace direct explanation.*

Characters often say less than they mean. That tension creates interest.

Prompt 15: Raise the Stakes

Prompt: *Suggest three ways this scene could become more difficult for the protagonist.*

Final Thoughts

Good fiction prompts do not replace storytelling. They sharpen it. Use AI to:

- brainstorm
- organize
- expand possibilities
- challenge assumptions

Do not hand it the steering wheel. You are still the driver.

Chapter 7
Memoir Prompts

A memoir is not autobiography. Autobiography often attempts to tell an entire life. A memoir usually focuses on meaning.

It asks:

- What happened?
- Why did it matter?
- Who was I then?
- Who did I become because of it?

AI can help memoir writers organize memories, identify themes, recover details, and discover connections. It cannot remember your life for you, but it can help you examine it.

Many memoir writers begin with the question: Do I have enough material for a book?

The answer is often yes. The challenge is rarely a lack of stories. The challenge is choosing which stories belong. These prompts are designed to help uncover experiences, identify emotional threads, and shape memories into narrative.

Memory Discovery Prompts

Prompt 1: Memory Mining

Prompt: *Help me brainstorm important memories related to* *[topic]. Ask follow-up questions that may uncover forgotten details.*

Examples

- childhood holidays
- military service
- teaching career
- caregiving

Sometimes memories return because another memory opens the door, or looking in detail at a memory can help shine new light on something.

Prompt 2: Timeline Builder

Prompt: *Help me create a timeline of important events related to this period of my life. Identify possible turning points and emotional milestones.*

Memoirs often become clearer when events are placed in order. One of the best uses for AI is quickly putting things in order and keeping track of them.

Prompt 3: Life Chapter Prompt

Prompt: *Divide this period of my life into possible "chapters." Suggest themes or lessons connected to each section.*

Example:

- Leaving home
- First job
- Marriage
- Loss
- Reinvention

Theme Discovery Prompts

Prompt 4: Finding the Real Story

Prompt: *Review these memories and identify possible themes, emotional arcs, or recurring patterns.*

Writers sometimes think their memoir is about raising children, for example, only to discover it is really about identity, or forgiveness, or resilience. While we usually discover these deeper themes while writing, finding them earlier makes for much less rewriting.

Prompt 5: Emotional Thread Prompt

Prompt: *Identify emotions that repeat across these memories and suggest how they may connect.*

This helps reveal narrative unity.

Prompt 6: Transformation Prompt

Prompt: *Compare who I was at the beginning of this experience to who I became afterward.*

Change creates memoirs. Transformation creates story.

Sensory Memory Prompts

Prompt 7: Recovering Details

Prompt: *Ask questions to help me remember sensory details about this event.*

Include:

- *sights*
- *sounds*
- *smells*
- *textures*
- *weather*

- *objects*
- *clothing*
- *surroundings*

Small details often carry emotional power.

Prompt 8: Place Memory Prompt

Prompt: *Help me describe this location as I remember it. Ask questions that recover atmosphere and sensory experience.*

Examples:

- Old kitchens
- School hallways
- Church basements
- Family farms
- Places matter

Prompt 9: Object Memory Prompt

Prompt: *Help me explore memories connected to this object and why it mattered.*

Examples:

- Wedding ring
- Cookbook
- Military medal
- Sewing box
- Photograph

Objects frequently become anchors in memoirs.

Narrative Structure Prompts

Prompt 10: Scene Selection

Prompt: *Review these memories and suggest which events should become full scenes and which could remain summary.*

Not every memory needs a chapter. Some deserve pages.

Others need only a paragraph.

Prompt 11: Central Question Prompt

Prompt: *Based on these experiences, suggest possible central questions that might drive the memoir.*

Examples:

- How do we survive grief?
- What does home mean?
- Can forgiveness rebuild a family?

Prompt 12: Ending Reflection Prompt

Prompt: *Suggest possible reflective endings that show growth without sounding overly sentimental.*

Memoir endings often look forward while honoring the past.

Difficult Memories

Some memoir material involves grief, trauma, illness, loss, or family conflict. AI may help organize these experiences.

It should not replace counseling, therapy, or professional support. Write carefully. Take breaks when needed. Your well-being matters more than finishing a chapter.

Final Thoughts

Memoirs begin with memory, but memory alone is not enough. Memoirs ask writers to find meaning. AI cannot do that work. Only the author can. AI may help uncover the path. You still walk it.

Chapter 8
Nonfiction Prompts

Nonfiction writers solve problems. Sometimes they teach. Sometimes they inspire. Sometimes they explain complex ideas in ways readers can understand.

Unlike fiction, which often begins with characters and conflict, nonfiction frequently begins with information. The challenge is turning information into a story readers actually want to finish.

AI can help nonfiction writers brainstorm topics, organize material, clarify ideas, identify reader questions, and strengthen structure. It cannot replace expertise.

If you are writing about history, medicine, law, finance, science, or any specialized field, accuracy still belongs to the author.

Use AI as an assistant. Not as a fact checker. Never assume the first answer is automatically correct.

Book Planning Prompts

Prompt 1: Define the Reader

Prompt: *Describe the ideal reader for this book. Include their goals, frustrations, experience level, and what problem they hope to solve.*

A book for beginners looks very different from a book for professionals. Knowing the reader changes everything. AI is an excellent way to help define your reader. Don't forget to consider age, occupation, and what other interests your target readers might share. The more information you have on your target reader, the better your book.

Prompt 2: Book Purpose Prompt

Prompt: *Help me define the purpose of this nonfiction book. What transformation or result should readers experience by the end?*

Ask: What will readers know? What will readers do? What will readers become?

Prompt 3: Table of Contents Builder

Prompt: *Create a possible table of contents for a book about [topic]. Organize it from beginner concepts to advanced material.*

Ask for:

- Short version
- Detailed version
- Workbook version
- Companion edition

One idea may support multiple products.

Research and Organization Prompts

Prompt 4: Research Questions Prompt

Prompt: *Identify important questions readers may ask about this topic.*

Examples:

- What mistakes do beginners make?
- What myths exist?
- What terminology should readers know?
- What objections might readers have?

Reader questions often become chapter headings.

Prompt 5: Topic Expansion Prompt

Prompt: *List subtopics, supporting ideas, examples, and related concepts connected to this topic.*

This works especially well when a chapter feels too short.

Prompt 6: Missing Information Prompt

Prompt: *Review this outline and identify places where readers may need additional explanation, examples, or definitions.*

Writers know their subject. Readers may not.

Teaching Prompts

Prompt 7: Explain for Different Audiences

Prompt: *Explain this concept for:*

- A beginner
- An intermediate reader
- An advanced reader

Teaching level matters. Too advanced loses readers. Too simple loses credibility.

Prompt 8: Example Generator

Prompt: *Suggest examples showing how this concept works in practice.*

Readers remember examples more easily than definitions.

Prompt 9: Analogy Prompt

Prompt: *Suggest analogies that simplify this topic without changing its meaning.*

Good analogies make difficult subjects easier.

Reader Engagement Prompts

Prompt 10: Reader Objections

Prompt: *Identify reasons readers may resist this advice and suggest ways to address those concerns.*

People rarely reject information. They reject uncertainty.

Prompt 11: Action Step Builder

Prompt: *Create practical exercises or action items readers can complete after this chapter.*

Good nonfiction encourages action.

Prompt 12: Reflection Questions

Prompt: *Create reflection questions readers can answer after reading this section.*

Useful for:

- Self-help
- Memoir-adjacent nonfiction
- Workbooks
- Business books
- Educational titles

Revision Prompts for Nonfiction

Prompt 13: Clarity Review

Prompt: *Review this section for places where explanations may confuse readers.*

Ask AI to identify:

- Unclear language
- Missing definitions
- Jargon
- Abrupt transitions

Prompt 14: Repetition Review

Prompt: *Identify repeated ideas, examples, or explanations.*

Nonfiction often repeats without the writer noticing.

Prompt 15: Reader Flow Prompt

Prompt: *Review this chapter and identify where readers may stop, lose interest, or need stronger transitions.*

Information alone does not hold attention. Flow matters.

Specialized Nonfiction Ideas

These prompts adapt easily for different categories.

Business

Suggest case studies, examples, and practical applications for this topic.

History

Identify events, people, timelines, and historical context that may require additional explanation.

Self-Help

Suggest exercises, reflections, and implementation steps.

Writing Books

Help organize this topic into lessons, examples, exercises, and reader takeaways.

Educational Material

Convert this information into teaching modules or lesson sequences.

Final Thoughts

Nonfiction is more than information. Readers can find information anywhere. What they need is guidance. AI can help organize knowledge. It can suggest structure. It can identify gaps. Expertise still comes from the author. Your experience remains the value. AI simply helps present it more clearly.

Chapter 9

Editing and Revision Prompts

Some writers assume AI is mainly useful during brainstorming. I often find it more useful during revision. Ideas are exciting. Editing is where books improve.

AI can help identify repetition, pacing problems, missing information, weak transitions, inconsistent characterization, structural issues, and areas needing clarification. Notice what I did ***not*** say. AI does not decide whether your book is good. It does not become your editor. And it certainly should not replace human judgment.

Think of AI as a second pair of eyes. Helpful. Fast. Occasionally wrong. Always in need of supervision.

The prompts in this chapter focus on improving existing work rather than generating new material.

Big Picture Revision Prompts

Prompt 1: Developmental Review

Prompt: *Review this chapter and identify possible issues with structure, pacing, clarity, emotional development, or organization.*

Ask for:

- Major issues first
- Minor issues second

- Examples only when needed

Large problems should be fixed before commas.

Prompt 2: Missing Scene Prompt

Prompt: *Review this section and identify places where additional scenes, examples, explanations, or transitions may help.*

Sometimes the problem is not what exists; it is what is missing.

Prompt 3: Reader Confusion Prompt

Prompt: *Identify places where readers may become confused or require additional explanation.*

Writers know their story so well sometimes they forget their readers do not.

Line Editing Prompts

Prompt 4: Repetition Finder

Prompt: *Identify repeated words, phrases, ideas, or descriptions.*

Every writer has favorites. Revision usually finds them. And AI is better at finding them than any other way I've tried.

Prompt 5: Overwriting Review

Prompt: *Identify places where wording could be simplified without losing meaning.*

Remember the comedian Tim Allen and his phrase "more power?" It works about as well in writing as it did on a comedy show. More words aren't always better.

Prompt 6: Underwriting Review

Prompt: *Identify places that may need additional detail, emotion, explanation, or sensory description.*

Some scenes need trimming. Others need expansion. If there is one thing AI is, it is objective. You may love your words, but AI will tell you when they are just not working.

Prompt 7: Transition Review

Prompt: *Review paragraph and scene transitions. Identify abrupt shifts or missing connections.*

Readers should move smoothly from one thought to the next. Sudden changes of topic can make something more difficult to understand.

Fiction Revision Prompts

Prompt 8: Character Consistency

Prompt: *Review this chapter and identify actions, dialogue, or reactions that may feel inconsistent with the character.*

Characters should evolve, not randomly change.

Prompt 9: Dialogue Review

Prompt: *Review this dialogue for:*

- Excessive exposition
- Repeated speech patterns
- Missing subtext
- Unnatural phrasing

Dialogue should sound human, not like an interview transcript. Long expositions of the storyline disguised as dialogue usually feel unnatural.

Prompt 10: Pacing Analysis

Prompt: *Identify slow sections and explain why pacing may weaken.*

Ask AI to classify necessary pauses, emotional reflections, excessive explanations, and repeated information.

Slow is not always bad. Boring is.

Prompt 11: Conflict Review

Prompt: *Identify places where tension, stakes, conflict, or obstacles could increase.*

Stories move because something resists the protagonist.

Memoir Revision Prompts

Prompt 12: Emotional Distance Prompt

Prompt: *Review this section and identify places where emotional depth could increase.*

Memoirs improve when reflection deepens.

Prompt 13: Reflection Balance

Prompt: *Identify places where narrative and reflection feel unbalanced.*

If you have too much story, readers may miss the meaning. With too much reflection, they may miss the momentum.

Prompt 14: Memory Clarity Prompt

Prompt: *Identify places where readers may need additional context, timeline information, or explanation.*

The writer lived it. The reader did not. It is easy to skimp on explanation when you know a subject so well.

Nonfiction Revision Prompts

Prompt 15: Clarity Check

Prompt: *Review this chapter and identify unclear explanations, jargon, missing definitions, or confusing sections.*

Expert knowledge sometimes skips steps. That confuses

readers, particularly those who are unfamiliar with the subject.

Prompt 16: Reader Question Prompt

Prompt: *Identify questions readers may still have after reading this section.*

Unanswered questions often reveal missing content.

Prompt 17: Example Gap Prompt

Prompt: *Identify concepts that would benefit from examples, case studies, illustrations, or exercises.*

Examples make information stick.

Final Polish Prompts

Prompt 18: Chapter Summary Review

Prompt: *Summarize this chapter in three sentences. Compare that summary to my intended purpose.*

If the summary misses the point, the chapter may miss it too.

Prompt 19: Strength and Weakness Review

Prompt: *List three strengths and three possible improvement areas for this section.*

Balanced feedback helps. Pure praise rarely improves a manuscript.

Prompt 20: Final Readiness Prompt

Prompt: *Review this chapter as if you were a reader. Identify remaining issues before publication.*

Ask specifically for:

- Clarity and pacing
- Repetition
- Missing information
- Reader confusion

Final Thoughts

A word of caution. Sometimes, editing, either with AI or without it, can become addictive. You fix one thing. Then another. Then another. Finally, you realize you are changing words from the revision back to the original. And you realize while you have revised Chapter One twelve times, Chapter Two still does not exist.

Perfection is not the goal. Completion is. Eventually the manuscript has to leave your desk.

Revision is where rough drafts become books. AI may help identify problems. It may suggest solutions. It may point toward stronger choices.

Judgment still belongs to the writer. The final decision remains yours. Always.

Chapter 10

Graphics and Visual Prompts

Reading is a visual art. What we see matters. The look and feel of the words on the page matter. Graphics, from front cover to graphs, charts, and other illustrations matter.

Words are the heart of publishing, but readers see visuals first. The cover appears before the first page. A social media graphic appears before the click. A bookmark, map, logo, or advertisement may introduce readers to a book long before they ever meet the characters.

AI image tools have changed how many authors approach graphics. They can help generate ideas quickly, create concept images, explore visual styles, produce marketing material, and assist with planning. They have also created a debate. Questions about copyright, training material, artistic ownership, licensing, and ethics continue to evolve.

This chapter will not settle those debates. Instead, think of it as a practical guide for authors who want to use visual AI responsibly and thoughtfully. Use the tools. Learn the strengths. Understand the limits. Respect artists. And remember sometimes a professional designer is still the best choice.

Concept Art Prompts

Concept art helps authors visualize people, settings, clothing, architecture, creatures, and atmosphere. These images may never appear in the final book. Their purpose is inspiration. For you and your graphic designer. Before AI, I could never show an artist what was in my mind. Sometimes my words didn't work well, either.

Prompt 1: Character Visualization

Prompt: *Create concept art for a [character description]. Include clothing, mood, age range, and setting details.*

Concept art often helps authors notice details they had not considered.

Prompt 2: Setting Exploration

Prompt: *Generate visual inspiration for this location. Include architecture, landscape, weather, and emotional atmosphere.*

Examples:

- Haunted seaside village
- Mountain retreat
- Historical resort
- Futuristic city
- Small Southern town

Settings influence mood.

Prompt 3: Creature and World Design

Prompt: *Create visual concepts for creatures, magical races, symbols, or objects from this world.*

Useful for:

- Fantasy
- Science fiction
- Paranormal fiction
- Gaming projects

Maps and Worldbuilding Graphics

Many authors think visually. Maps help. Timelines help. Relationship charts help. Readers often enjoy them, too.

Prompt 4: Fantasy Map Prompt

Prompt: *Create a map showing terrain, settlements, roads, waterways, and important landmarks. Use a fantasy style.*

I've had trouble with AI created maps. When it gets it right the first time, it's great. The other times, getting it to change is very difficult. Sometimes it lists a specific place on a map more than once, "makes up" place names I haven't asked for, etc.

Prompt 5: Historical Location Prompt

Prompt: *Generate visual references for a location during [time period]. Include architecture, transportation, clothing, and atmosphere.*

Remember to always verify historical accuracy. AI may invent details.

Prompt 6: Symbol Design Prompt

Prompt: *Create symbolic designs representing cultures, factions, families, magical systems, organizations, or fictional groups.*

Readers remember symbols. Writers remember them too. Describing the family crest of a clan is fun but I want to see it, too. Both as a writer and a reader.

Author Branding Prompts

Graphics are not limited to books. Authors are brands. Even authors who dislike marketing usually discover they need visuals eventually. A logo, a business card, and a website header all need graphics.

Prompt 7: Brand Identity Prompt

Prompt: *Create branding ideas using these colors, themes, and audience expectations.*

Consider:

- Colors
- Fonts
- Symbols
- Mood
- Genre expectations

Prompt 8: Social Graphic Prompt

Prompt: *Create graphics promoting a book launch, preorder, newsletter signup, podcast appearance, or reader event.*

Possible uses:

- Facebook posts
- Instagram graphics
- Newsletters
- Event banners

Prompt 9: Background and Presentation Prompt

Prompt: *Create a virtual background suitable for interviews, webinars, podcasts, or livestreams.*

Include:

- Books
- Branding
- Subtle imagery
- Readable text areas

Interior Graphics and Extras

Visual material can strengthen a reader's experience. Examples include:

- Chapter graphics
- Dividers
- Maps
- Workbook pages
- Companion guides
- Family trees
- Timelines

Prompt 10: Chapter Decoration Prompt

Prompt: *Create simple decorative graphics matching the theme and tone of this book.*

Prompt 11: Companion Material Prompt

Prompt: *Design supporting graphics for worksheets, journals, guides, or bonus material.*

Prompt 12: Series Consistency Prompt

Prompt: *Create visual guidelines that keep covers, graphics, colors, and typography consistent across a series.*

Consistency helps recognition. Recognition helps readers to find the second, third, and later books in a series, and that creates fans!

Using AI Images Responsibly

AI graphics remain a developing field. Rules change. Platforms change. Technology changes.

Authors should pay attention to:

- Usage rights
- Licenses
- Platform restrictions
- Commercial permissions

- Attribution requirements
- Style imitation concerns

Avoid assuming an image is automatically safe for commercial use. Always verify.

When Human Artists Are Better

AI is fast, but human artists bring interpretation.

Consider hiring an artist when you need:

- Custom cover illustration
- Complex maps
- Highly detailed scenes
- Collector editions
- Licensed commercial work
- Brand identity systems

Sometimes the best prompt is: *I need an artist.* That is perfectly acceptable.

Final Thoughts

Graphics support books; they do not replace them. Use visual AI for inspiration. Use it for experimentation. Use it for planning. But remember: Readers stay for the story.

Chapter 11
Publishing Prompts

Finishing the manuscript is only part of publishing. As an author, you still face writing descriptions, choosing keywords and categories, worrying about metadata and formatting, planning your book launch, and a host of other questions.

Most of us enjoy writing books far more than we do publishing them. AI can help.

It cannot upload your book. It cannot guarantee sales. It cannot replace publishing knowledge. However, it can organize tasks, generate options, and save you time.

Book Positioning Prompts

Prompt 1: Reader Positioning

Prompt: *Identify the ideal audience for this book and explain why readers would choose it. Look at age, gender, income level, and other factors.*

Prompt 2: Comparable Titles

Prompt: *Suggest books that may appeal to readers of this title. Explain audience overlap.*

Prompt 3: Category Prompt

Prompt: *Suggest possible publishing categories for this* *book and explain the advantages of each.*

There are so many genres, sub-genres, and sub-sub-genres. It is impossible to be aware of them all. Amazon, which is arguably the most important place for categorizing your book, changes their categories periodically. AI can scan the categories and come up with several choices for you. It not only saves time, but it may help you find just the right category you didn't even know existed.

Prompt 4: Keyword Prompt

Prompt: *Generate search keywords readers might use to find books like this one.*

I've always hated finding keywords. There are a number of keyword generator products on the internet; some are better than others. AI is one of the best.

Product Description Prompts

Prompt 5: Back Cover Blurb

Prompt: *Write a back cover blurb emphasizing reader benefits and emotional appeal. Make sure it complies with current Amazon KDP algorithms.*

Why is it still called a back cover blurb when the first place it is used is your internet listing? I have no idea! But this is the most important piece of marketing you have. It's where people will make an almost instant decision whether to purchase your book or not. Writing a 100,000-word book and writing a 500-word description are separate skills.

Prompt 6: Short Description Prompt

Prompt: *Create a short promotional description under 100 words.*

Just when you've got that long description written to your

satisfaction, someone wants a shorter one. AI can cut out the dross and find the gold in that long description quickly and easily.

Prompt 7: Hook Prompt

Prompt: *Suggest opening hooks for a book description.*

Prompt 8: Tagline Prompt

Prompt: *Create possible taglines for this book.*

Back Matter Prompts

The popularity of e-books makes back matter more important than ever. Back matter is the variety of things an author puts at the back of the book. This can include a preview of another book, social media links, a list of other books written by the author, and a request for reviews. It should be used at the back of every e-book, and most of it should be adapted for paper books also. QR codes are a great help with this.

Prompt 9: Next Book Teaser

Prompt: *Write a teaser encouraging readers to continue the series.*

Prompt 10: Newsletter Invitation

Prompt: *Create a reader invitation encouraging newsletter signup.*

Prompt 11: Reader Review Request

Prompt: *Write a polite review request for the back matter.*

Reminding your readers to review your book is something you should do as often as possible.

Prompt 12: Bonus Material Prompt

Prompt: *Suggest reader extras such as maps, guides, recipes, glossaries, timelines, or companion material.*

Launch Preparation Prompts

I've always used the items in this list. Before AI, I had to make them for each book I worked on for myself and my clients. AI can do in a few minutes what I used to spend an hour or more doing.

Prompt 13: Launch Checklist

Prompt: *Create a publication checklist for e-book release.*

Prompt 14: Print Checklist

Prompt: *Create a print publishing checklist including formatting and proof review.*

Prompt 15: Launch Calendar

Prompt: *Create a one-year, six-month, and thirty-day launch schedule.*

Prompt 16: Problem Finder

Prompt: *Identify common publishing mistakes authors make before release.*

Chapter 12
Marketing Prompts

Marketing frightens many writers. Some avoid it; some postpone it. Some hope readers will magically appear. Unfortunately, books rarely market themselves. As one writer I know puts it, "I save my creativity for my writing and let my AI help me with marketing."

AI can help create ideas, schedules, posts, campaigns, and reader materials. It cannot replace relationships. Readers still connect with people, not algorithms.

Audience Prompts

Prompt 1: Reader Persona

Prompt: *Describe the ideal reader including interests, favorite books, age range, and buying habits.*

Prompt 2: Reader Pain Points

Prompt: *Identify reader problems, interests, hopes, or emotional needs.*

This is especially good for the nonfiction writer.

Prompt 3: Brand Voice Prompt

Prompt: *Help define a consistent author voice for marketing.*

Newsletter Prompts

Prompt 4: Newsletter Topics

Prompt: *Generate five newsletter ideas related to this genre or topic.*

Prompt 5: Welcome Series Prompt

Prompt: *Outline a welcome sequence for new subscribers.*

A welcome sequence is a series of emails automatically sent to new subscribers to introduce your brand, deliver freebies, build trust, and guide readers toward your books and products.

Prompt 6: Reader Magnet Prompt

Prompt: *Suggest bonus material readers may exchange for newsletter signup.*

Prompt 7: Re-engagement Prompt

Prompt: *Create ideas for reconnecting inactive subscribers.*

Social Media Prompts

Prompt 8: Social Calendar

Prompt: *Create thirty days of social media ideas.*

Prompt 9: Book Launch Posts

Prompt: *Generate launch posts for multiple platforms.*

Prompt 10: Reader Engagement Prompt

Prompt: *Suggest questions that encourage reader interaction.*

Prompt 11: Behind-the-Scenes Prompt

Prompt: *Generate ideas showing writing process, research, or worldbuilding.*

Prompt 12: Repurpose Prompt

Prompt: *Convert one long article into multiple social posts.*

Advertising Prompts

Prompt 13: Ad Hook Prompt

Prompt: *Generate attention hooks for book advertising.*

Prompt 14: Benefit Prompt

Prompt: *Identify emotional benefits readers receive.*

Prompt 15: Seasonal Prompt

Prompt: *Suggest marketing tied to holidays, seasons, or events.*

Prompt 16: Promotion Prompt

Prompt: *Brainstorm promotional ideas for a limited-time sale.*

Final Thoughts

AI may help create ideas, but if you don't follow through and do the work, the ideas are useless. AI can generate a social media calendar. You still have to set up the posts. AI can give you great marketing ideas, but unless you follow through and set up the campaigns, you'll never know if they work.

Chapter 13

Combining Prompts for Better Results

Working with AI is a process. Beginners often write one prompt; experienced users build conversations. Large projects usually require multiple steps. Think of it as a series of questions and answers: Ask a prompt; get a response. After reading the answer, refine the first prompt and ask again. Now, expand the prompt, review, revise, and continue to ask questions until you have the ideas and information that you need.

In this chapter we will talk about how to do just that: combine earlier prompts into workflows to help you continue the conversation.

Workflow 1: Fiction Novel

Prompt 1: *Generate five story ideas.*

Prompt 2: *Expand the strongest idea.*

Prompt 3: *Suggest opening conflict.*

Prompt 4: *Create character goals and fears.*

Prompt 5: *Identify major turning points.*

Prompt 6: *Review for missing tension.*

Workflow 2: Memoir

Prompt 7: *Brainstorm memories around a topic.*

Prompt 8: *Identify themes.*

Prompt 9: *Create emotional timeline.*
Prompt 10 : *Suggest chapter divisions.*
Prompt 11 : *Identify transformation.*
Prompt 12: *Review emotional balance.*

Workflow 3: Nonfiction Book

Prompt 13: *Define reader.*
Prompt 14: *Create outline.*
Prompt 15: *Identify reader questions.*
Prompt 16: *Expand lessons.*
Prompt 17: *Add examples.*
Prompt 18: *Review clarity.*

Workflow 4: Revision Pass

Prompt 19: *Review structure.*
Prompt 20: *Check pacing.*
Prompt 21: *Find repetition.*
Prompt 22: *Identify reader confusion.*
Prompt 23: *Review strengths.*
Prompt 24: *Prepare final review.*

Workflow 5: Book Launch

Prompt 25: *Create keywords.*
Prompt 26: *Write description.*
Prompt 27: *Develop launch schedule.*
Prompt 28: *Create newsletter.*
Prompt 29: *Generate social content.*
Prompt 30: *Review campaign.*

Building Your Own Workflow

Our brains, or at least my brain, rarely functions in as organized a way as these workflow prompts show. The answer to one prompt sends me on a different tangent. The realities of day-to-day life interfere, and I leave the project for a few hours or days.

The great thing about AI is when you turn it off, it waits patiently for you to get back to work and picks up where you left off.

Different AI software has different methods of saving or deleting your chats. Make sure you label and save them so you can easily find them again after you've taken a break from a particular project.

The sequences I suggest do not need to be used in exactly these orders. Change them, add or remove steps, combine them in different ways. The best systems are personal.

Prompting is not magic. It is a process. Small steps become larger projects, questions become books, and conversations become tools.

Part 3

Working Like an Authorpreneur

How AI Helps You as an Authorpreneur

Writing a book is only part of modern authorship.

Today's writers often become publishers, marketers, newsletter creators, product developers, speakers, teachers, and business owners. Many of us never expected all that. We imagined writing life as books, coffee, and inspiration. We discovered spreadsheets, metadata, newsletters, launch calendars, and social media somewhere along the way.

Years ago, I began telling authors that I was looking for writers with an entrepreneurial spirit. Eventually I discovered there was already a word for it: *Authorpreneur.*

An Authorpreneur is more than someone who writes books. An Authorpreneur understands writing and publishing are connected. Creating the work matters. Helping readers discover it matters, too.

The goal is not to become a marketing machine.

The goal is to build a sustainable writing life.

AI can help with that.

It cannot replace judgment, or creativity, or experience, but it can become another tool in your author toolbox.

This section moves beyond writing prompts and into something larger:

How serious authors use AI to work like Authorpreneurs.

Chapter 14

Advanced Prompting: Moving Beyond Basic Requests

You understand prompt structure. You know prompts need goals, context, roles, constraints, and output. You know wording changes results. You know prompting works best as a conversation rather than a single question. Now, we move to the next level.

Advanced prompting is not about writing longer prompts. It is about thinking more intentionally. Experienced AI users rarely ask one question and accept one answer. They build layers. They challenge responses. They refine these ideas. They ask AI to examine assumptions, compare possibilities, and improve earlier work.

In short, they prompt like editors. And writers. And Authorpreneurs.

Prompt Layering

As we talked about in Chapter Three, prompt layering means building information one step at a time. Instead of a **Weak Prompt:** *Help me plan my fantasy novel,* try:

Prompt 1: *Suggest three fantasy concepts involving hidden magical communities.*

Prompt 2: *Expand idea two.*

Prompt 3: *Increase political conflict.*

Prompt 4: *Add romantic tension.*
Prompt 5: *Suggest a midpoint reversal.*

Each answer becomes material for the next. You are building, not downloading. Prompt layering works especially well for novels, memoir timelines, nonfiction outlines, book launches, reader magnets, marketing campaigns, and more.

Large projects become easier when divided into pieces.

Role Stacking

Earlier we assigned AI one role at a time, such as developmental editor or marketing consultant. Advanced prompting combines roles. Here's an example;

Prompt 6: *Act as both a developmental editor and reader psychologist. Review this chapter for emotional tension and identify places readers may disengage.*

Or:

Prompt 7: *Respond as a publishing consultant and newsletter strategist. Suggest launch ideas for this nonfiction book.*

Role stacking creates broader viewpoints, but use it carefully. Too many roles at one time create confusion. For you and AI. Two or three usually work best.

Constraint Chains

Beginning users often use one instruction at a time. Advanced users build boundaries. For example:

Prompt 8: *Review this chapter for pacing problems.*

Now add:

- Preserve character voice
- Do not alter plot events
- Limit suggestions to three

- Focus only on emotional pacing
- Ignore grammar

Suddenly the request becomes precise.

Constraints tell AI what matters, and just as important, it tells it what does not.

Ask AI to Challenge Itself

One of the most useful advanced techniques is asking AI to critique its own answer. Try:

- Identify weaknesses in your previous response.
- What assumptions did you make?
- Which suggestions rely on guesswork?
- What evidence supports this conclusion?
- Offer an alternative interpretation.

This works especially well for:

- Plot development
- Nonfiction organization
- Marketing plans
- Reader targeting
- Revisions

AI often improves when it is asked to question itself. Writers do the same thing with every revision pass.

Reverse Prompting

Sometimes asking for the opposite reveals more. Suppose you ask: *Increase romantic tension.* Try reversing it.

Prompt 9: *Identify what currently reduces romantic tension.*

Or instead of: *Strengthen my marketing,* ask *What marketing mistakes might weaken this launch?*

Instead of *improve pacing,* ask, *What causes this chapter to slow?*

Reverse prompts uncover hidden problems.

The Refinement Loop

Professional prompting often looks like this:

- Create
- Review
- Question
- Refine
- Repeat

For example:

Prompt 10: *Create six newsletter ideas for indie authors.*

Prompt 11: *Organize them into a six-week sequence.*

Prompt 12: *Identify which topics should promote books, products, or services.*

Prompt 13: *Add reader actions or calls to action.*

Prompt 14: *Repurpose each into social media posts.*

This isn't one prompt; it's a workflow, and workflows are where serious users often get their best results.

When Short Prompts Work Better

I've mentioned this before: advanced prompts don't necessarily mean longer prompts.

Sometimes this works: *Increase tension.* It might be all you need. But sometimes this works better: *Increase romantic tension while preserving dialogue.* You've asked a different question, and you may get a much different response.

There are times when you need detail. Advanced prompting is choosing the right amount. Not the biggest amount. You need enough information, not ***all*** the information.

Final Thoughts

Advanced prompting is not about becoming more technical; it is about becoming more deliberate. You already know how to do this. Writers revise. Editors question. Publishers organize.

Authorpreneurs combine all three.

AI simply gives you another way to continue the conversation.

Exercise

Take one prompt from Part Two.

Improve it using:

1. Prompt layering
2. A second role
3. Two new constraints
4. A follow-up critique prompt

Save the result.

You have just created your first advanced workflow.

Chapter 15
AI Across the Author Business

Many authors first meet AI while writing. They ask for character ideas. Scene suggestions. Plot twists. Blurb help. Then one day they realize something surprising: writing may only be ten percent of their job. The rest is newsletters. Social media. Back cover copy. Reader magnets. Launch plans. Websites. Metadata. Keywords. Events. Podcasts. Advertising. Tracking sales. Updating books. Managing readers.

Welcome to the authorpreneur life.

AI can help with much of this work, but only if you ask the right questions. This chapter is not about asking AI to *run* your business. It is about using AI to support the business you already run.

Authors Have Many Jobs

Most authors wear more hats than they ever thought they'd need:

- Writer
- Editor
- Publisher
- Graphics coordinator

- Newsletter creator
- Social media manager
- Ad tester
- Event planner
- Website updater
- Accountant
- Customer service department

AI can assist in many of these roles. Note the word *assist.* While I often wish someone would just take over my business and do it for me, AI isn't there yet. Our goal in asking AI for help with our author business is not replacement, it's support.

Example Workflow: Building a Newsletter Plan

A beginner prompt often looks like this: *Write my newsletter.*

That may produce something usable. It may also produce something generic. A workflow often works better.

Prompt 1: *Create six newsletter ideas for indie authors.*

Prompt 2: *Organize them into a six-week sequence.*

Prompt 3: *Identify which topics promote books, products, or services.*

Prompt 4: *Add reader actions or calls to action.*

Prompt 5: *Repurpose each into social media posts.*

Notice what happened. You did not ask for one finished item. You built a system.

Professional prompting often becomes workflow design.

Example Workflow: Preparing a Book Launch

Prompting can also support launches.

Try something like:

Prompt 6: *Create a launch checklist for an indie fantasy novel.*

Prompt 7: *Divide tasks into prelaunch, launch week, and postlaunch.*

Prompt 8: *Identify which tasks require graphics.*

Prompt Four: *Suggest newsletter timing.*

Prompt Five: *Recommend social media variations.*

The result is not merely content. It is organization. And organization saves time.

Example Workflow: Working Across Multiple Books

Many authors do not have one project. They have five. Or ten. Or a folder labeled *Someday.*

AI can help organize:

- Series planning.
- Shared universes.
- Character tracking.
- Research notes.
- Marketing calendars.
- Back matter updates.
- Reader bonus ideas.
- Spin-offs and companion books.

The larger your writing world becomes, the more useful systems become.

A Note About Delegation

You will sometimes hear people say, "AI wrote my newsletter." Or, "AI wrote my social posts." Or, "AI wrote my ad copy."

You may choose that path. You may not. That decision belongs to you. Keep in mind readers often connect with *your voice.* Your experience, your stories, your mistakes, your opinions.

AI can help organize those things. It cannot live them.

Exercise

Choose one part of your author business.

Examples:

- Newsletter planning.
- Website updates.
- Launch preparation.
- Reader magnets.
- Podcast appearances.
- Advertising.
- Metadata.
- Social media.

Create a five-step workflow instead of one prompt.

Ask:

- Create
- Review
- Question
- Refine

Repeat

Congratulations! You are no longer simply prompting. You are designing systems.

Chapter 16

Ethics, Limits, and Human Judgment

You have seen what prompts can do. You used prompts to brainstorm, organize, outline, edit, market, research, and build systems around your writing life. You learned strong prompts often come from conversations, refinement, and workflows rather than from one perfect question.

This is where many books stop, but you should not. Sooner or later every author reaches the moment where AI gives them an answer, and they think:

That sounds right… but is it? Or: *I don't think my character would do that.* Or: *This feels wrong.*

Those moments matter. AI is powerful. It is not human. And authors still provide the judgment.

AI Is a Tool, Not an Authority

One of the easiest mistakes to make is assuming confidence equals accuracy. AI uses a calm, professional voice. It may sound certain. It may sound intelligent. It may even sound convincing.

That does not automatically make it correct.

Professional users question, verify, edit. In other words, they think for themselves. Treat AI more like an enthusiastic assistant than an expert witness.

Useful? Absolutely. Always correct? No.

Hallucinations Happen

In AI discussions you may hear the term, "hallucination,". No, the software is not seeing purple dragons—although that is probably possible.

A hallucination is information that sounds believable but is incorrect, invented, incomplete, or misleading.

For example, AI may invent book references and give incorrect historical details, fake citations, wrong dates, imaginary research sources, made-up quotes, character continuity errors, or false assumptions about your story.

Prompt example:

Weak Prompt: *Tell me everything about Victorian mourning customs.*

Possible result: You receive ten paragraphs. Nine are right. One is completely wrong. And unless you already know the subject, you may never notice.

Better Prompt: *Summarize Victorian mourning customs and identify any areas that should be independently verified.* It's a small change but a much safer result.

AI Will Ask Questions Too

Many authors expect prompting to work like pressing a button—ask, receive, done.

As we covered in Chapter Four, real use often looks different. You ask. AI answers. AI asks for clarification. You refine. It responds again. That is normal progression. Here's another example:

Author: Help me create a newsletter.

AI: Who is the audience?

Author: Indie authors.

AI: Beginning authors or experienced publishers?

Author: Mostly self-publishing writers.

The conversation continues. Those questions are not failures. They are often the system trying to narrow the task. Good prompts reduce guessing. Questions reduce mistakes. Sometimes the fastest path is answering one extra question.

Copyright, Ownership, and Responsibility

Laws about AI continue to evolve. Platforms change, policies change, and the tools change.

The safest assumption is simple. Review everything. Edit everything. Make the work yours. Do not blindly paste something. Do not publish without reading. Do not assume AI-generated material is automatically correct, original, or safe.

If you use AI images, research current platform policies. If you quote material, verify sources. If you publish nonfiction, check facts. If you write memoir, protect privacy. Professional prompting includes responsibility. That responsibility belongs to you, not to AI.

Sensitive Material and Boundaries

Authors write about difficult things such as violence, trauma, and personal experiences. Almost anything you write could be a trigger for someone else. AI tools may respond differently depending on subject matter.

Some requests are limited. Some receive warnings. Some are rewritten. Some are refused. This is not necessarily the system "breaking." It may be following safety guidelines written into its software. When that happens, try reframing the prompt. Add context and clarify purpose.

Explain the material is for fiction, memoir, editing, or analysis. Often wording changes improve results.

When to Ignore AI

This may be the most important prompt skill in the entire book. Ignore bad advice. Ignore generic advice. Ignore edits that remove your voice. Ignore ideas that do not fit your audience.

AI does not know your entire career. You do. Sometimes the best prompt response is: *No thank you.*

Professional users reject ideas all the time.

Prompting is not surrendering decisions. It is improving conversations. AI may help create faster. It may help organize better. It may help brainstorm farther.

The writer still decides what belongs on the page. You are not replacing judgment. You are using it.

Exercise

Take one AI response you created earlier.

Ask:

1. What parts are correct?
2. What should be verified?
3. What reflects my voice?
4. What feels generic?
5. What should be rewritten?
6. What would I remove entirely?
7. What did I contribute that AI could not?

Your answers matter more than the original output.

Chapter 17

Building Your Personal Prompt Library

Stop reinventing every prompt. The best prompt is often one you already used.

Many new AI users write prompts one at a time. Need a blurb? Write a prompt. Need editing help? Write another. Need social posts? Start over. Need newsletter ideas? Start over again.

It works. Eventually most serious users discover they keep asking for the same things over and over. Names change, books change, projects change, but the prompts stay surprisingly similar.

That is when a prompt library becomes useful.

What Is a Prompt Library?

A prompt library is simply a collection of prompts you save and reuse. Nothing fancy, no special software required. A notebook or Word document works.

The goal is simple: Stop rebuilding what already works. Think of it as creating your own prompting toolbox.

Save the Winners

Not every prompt deserves a permanent home. Some are one-time experiments. Some fail or become outdated.

Save the prompts that repeatedly help. For example, character interviews, conflict builders, scene expansion prompts, memoir memory prompts are all writing prompts you will use over and over again.

You will find other prompts for editing, marketing, and business that work consistently for you.

One mistake authors make is saving only the prompt itself. Months later they look at it and wonder why it worked. Instead, save the prompt name, the prompt itself, and a few notes on how you used it.

Version Numbers Are Your Friends

Prompts evolve; the first version may be good, the fifth version may be excellent.

Example:

Version 1: *Review this chapter.*

Too broad.

Version 2: *Review this chapter for pacing.*

Better.

Version 3: *Review this chapter for pacing only. Identify slow sections and explain why readers may lose tension.*

Much stronger. Save the improvements. Your prompt library should grow smarter over time.

Create Prompt Workflows

Professional users often keep workflows instead of single prompts. For example:

Newsletter Workflow

Prompt 1: *Generate five newsletter topics for indie authors.*

Prompt 2: *Rank by likely reader interest.*

Prompt 3: *Expand the strongest topic.*

Prompt 4: *Create a four-week content schedule.*

Prompt 5: *Adapt for social media.*

One task. Multiple prompts. Better results.

Organize by Project Type

Many authors eventually divide prompts by purpose. Possible folders include:

Fiction: divided into:

- Characters
- Worldbuilding
- Conflict etc.

Memoir:

- Memory recovery prompts
- Timeline building, Interview questions
- Research prompts
- Theme
- Reflection exercises

Nonfiction:

- Lesson planning
- Teaching examples
- Chapter organization
- Workbook ideas
- Reader questions

Publishing and Marketing:

- Blurbs
- Keywords
- Newsletter content
- Book descriptions
- Reader magnets etc.

Author Business:

- Scheduling
- Goal reviews
- Time management
- Income ideas
- Delegation
- Workflow creation

Build a "Use Often" Folder

Every writer develops favorites.

Mine include:

- Newsletter creation
- Worldbuilding
- Book organization.

Yours may be:

- Character interviews
- Historical research
- Scene expansion.

Keep frequently used prompts together. You should not need to search through fifty files to find your top five tools.

Retire Old Prompts

AI changes, and we change, too. Models improve. Workflows evolve. Some prompts become unnecessary. Occasionally review what to keep, what to improve or rewrite, what to delete. Your prompt library is a living document. Treat it like one.

Prompting becomes easier when you stop starting from zero. Save good prompts. Improve them. Organize them. Keep notes. Over time your library becomes more than prompts. It becomes experience.

Exercise: Start Your Library

Create four folders.

1. Writing
2. Editing
3. Marketing
4. Business

Now save:

- Three prompts you already use
- One workflow
- One prompt you want to improve

Congratulations!
You now have a prompt library.
Professional users often start exactly this way.

Chapter 18

The Future of Prompting for Authors

By now you have probably noticed something. This book is not really about prompts. Not entirely.

It is about learning to work with AI. Prompts are the language we use to do that. And that language is changing quickly. New tools appear. Old tools disappear. Features move. Policies change. Interfaces update. Entire companies seem to rise and fall overnight. Trying to predict every change would be impossible. Some trends are already visible.

Prompting Becomes More Conversational

Early AI users often treated prompting like coding, probably because most of them were coders. The prompts were very precise, technical, and structured. Sometimes prompting still works that way.

Increasingly, however, AI tools behave more like conversations; you ask, and it answers. You refine; it asks questions. You redirect and continue.

Professional prompting is less about writing one perfect instruction and more about managing an ongoing discussion.

That shift matters. Authors already know how to have conversations. We do it every time we write dialogue.

AI Is Expanding Beyond Text

Many authors first meet AI through writing, but it no longer stops there. As discussed in this book, it now can assist with a wide variety of publishing and marketing tasks. Some authors will use only text tools. Others will build entire businesses around AI-assisted production. Neither approach is wrong. Use what works for you and ignore what does not.

This book began with prompts and ends with systems. Increasingly, experienced users think in workflows. The individual prompt matters. The process often matters more.

Human Skills Become More Valuable

This surprises people. Many assume AI reduces the value of writers. I suspect the opposite may happen. As more content appears, readers may value human perspective more. Experience, emotion, voice, and judgment are all difficult things to automate.

A memoir written from lived experience still matters. A novel shaped by years of imagination still matters. Teaching built from expertise still matters. AI can help organize. It cannot live your life.

The Writer's Job Is Changing

Authors today are more than writers; they are authorpreneurs wearing many hats, from writer, to publisher, to marketer, and more. AI can reduce some of that workload by speeding up certain tasks and simplifying repetitive work. It also asks authors to learn new skills. Prompting becomes one of them.

The one thing AI cannot do is make sure you follow through with the plans, the schedules, the marketing, and the writing it helped you to brainstorm and organize. No matter how great the AI plan, if you, the human author, don't follow through, all the plans in the world are meaningless.

You Do Not Need to Learn Everything

I learned a lesson many years ago when I was a stay-at-home mom and wanted to get back into the workplace. I was afraid technology had passed me by. I confided this to a former coworker, and he gave me excellent advice, "You don't have to worry about everything you've missed. Technology is changing so quickly we all need to master something new every few years. Don't worry about what you've missed, only about what you need today."

AI is just another part of that evolution. You don't need to master every AI tool, every image generator, or chatbot, or even every update. Find what works for you and ignore the rest.

The goal is not to use more AI; it is to write better, work smarter, save time, stay creative, and finish projects. AI is one possible path toward those goals, not the destination.

Prompting will change; tools will change; publishing will change. Writers always adapt.

We moved from typewriters to word processors, from paper submissions to digital publishing, from bookstores to online retailers. Now we add AI, not instead of writing, but alongside it. The story continues.

Exercise: Looking Forward

Ask yourself what part of writing takes the most energy? What task do I avoid? What work repeats every month? What process could become easier? What still needs *me*?

Those answers may shape your future prompt library more than any trend.

Chapter 19

Keeping Your Voice in an AI World

If you spend enough time around discussions of AI, eventually you will hear the question, *Will AI replace writers?* It appears in interviews, social media posts, writing groups, and publishing conferences.

Writers care deeply about words. We spend years learning our craft. Then suddenly a machine arrives producing pages in seconds. That is enough to make anyone pause.

People often talk about voice as if it means word choice. It is larger than that. Voice is experience and perspective. It is what the writer notices: the details they choose, the memories they share, the questions they ask.

Two writers with the same prompt will produce entirely different books. Why? Because the writer still matters. A memoir written by someone who lived the events cannot be duplicated by software. A novel built from years of imagination carries the fingerprints of the author. Even nonfiction reflects teaching style, priorities, and lived knowledge.

AI can help organize ideas. It cannot become you.

Exercise: Define Your Voice

Write answers to these questions:

- What subjects do I return to repeatedly?
- What themes appear in my work?
- What experiences shape my writing?
- What emotions do I explore most?
- What makes my books recognizable?

Continue Your AI Journey

Want to Go Deeper?

Prompt Like a Pro teaches you how to speak to AI. *AI for Authors: An Almost Up-to-Date Guide* explores the tools themselves.

Inside you will find:

- AI programs for writers
- Editing and research tools
- Publishing applications
- Marketing uses
- Ethics and limitations
- Ways to keep your own voice while using AI

Together, the books form a companion set for authors working in fiction, nonfiction, memoir, publishing, and author business.

Reader Bonus

Free Companion Download

Prompt Like a Pro: 30 High-Impact Prompts for Serious Authors

Download a free companion guide featuring additional prompts, workflow ideas, and practical examples designed for working writers. Plus receive updates, articles, and resources for independent authors.

Visit: Open Door Publications Newsletter signup page (You can insert final URL later.)

Continue the Conversation

Writing changes. Publishing changes. AI changes every few months. Authors adapt.

Join Karen's newsletter for:

✓ AI updates for writers.

✓ Publishing tips.

✓ Self-publishing strategies.

✓ Marketing ideas.

✓ New releases from Open Door Publications.

Continue Your AI Journey

If you found **Prompt Like a Pro** helpful, you may enjoy the companion guide:
AI for Authors: An Almost Up-to-Date Guide
Inside you'll discover:
• Reviews of major AI writing tools
• Ethical and legal considerations for authors
• Privacy and security issues when using AI
• Interviews with working writers using AI today
• Practical strategies for integrating AI into your writing workflow
AI is not about replacing authors.
It's about helping serious authors work smarter.

More Books in the "You Can Do This!" Series

Self-Publishing: You Can Do This!
A clear roadmap for navigating the modern self-publishing world.
Authorpreneur: Build the Business Behind the Book
Learn how authors build sustainable publishing careers.
Memoir Made Easy
A practical guide for organizing and writing the story of your life.

Also by Karen Hodges Miller

Hibiscus Strong An award-winning memoir, set in Florida, about resilience, family, and rebuilding. A deeply personal story of strength, healing, and the determination to move forward.

Writing as Lee K. Rogers

The Hunter's Moon
The Artificial Witch
The Wolf Revealed

About the Author

Karen Hodges Miller is an author, editor, and publishing consultant with more than thirty years of experience in journalism and book publishing. She is the founder and CEO of **Open Door Publications**, a company dedicated to helping authors successfully write, publish, and market their books in the modern publishing landscape.

She has written more than ten books in both fiction and nonfiction. Her publishing guides include *How to Sell Your Book Today*, *Self-Publishing: You Can Do This!*, and *Authorpreneur: Build the Business Behind the Book.*

Her memoir, *Hibiscus Strong*, received a **Gold Medal from The Bookfest** and a **Silver Medal from the Florida Authors and Publishers Association.**

Karen also writes paranormal romance under the name **Lee K. Rogers**.

Connect with Karen

OpenDoorPublications.com
KarenHodgesMiller.com
LeeKRogersAuthor.com
You can also connect with Karen on **LinkedIn and Facebook** for writing tips, publishing insights, and upcoming workshops.

Learn With Karen

Karen regularly teaches workshops for writers including:
- **Prompt Like a Pro**
- **AI for Authors**
- **Memoir Made Easy**
- **Why You Should Write a Book**

Visit OpenDoorPublications.com and sign up for her newsletter to get updates on upcoming events.

If you found this guide helpful, explore:

AI for Authors: An Almost Up-to-Date Guide

Inside you'll find:

- In-depth app reviews.
- Ethical and legal considerations.
- Interviews with working authors.
- Privacy guidance.
- Advanced AI strategy.

AI is not about replacing authors, it is about helping serious authors work smarter.

Enjoyed This Book?

Reviews help more authors discover independent publishing resources. If *Prompt Like a Pro* helped you think differently about AI, consider leaving a review. Even a few sentences make a difference.

Thank you for reading.

www.ingramcontent.com/pod-product-compliance
Lightning Source LLC
LaVergne TN
LVHW022105200926
848481LV00003B/1066

* 9 7 9 8 9 8 7 1 6 9 7 9 7 *